APES

AND OTHER HAIRY PRIMATES

APES
AND OTHER HAIRY PRIMATES

By
Richard Platt

Consultant
David Burnie

A Dorling Kindersley Book

INTRODUCTION

Coming face to face with a monkey or an ape is an experience you won't easily forget. In a forest clearing, in a wildlife park or zoo, even on film or TV – it doesn't matter where. Stare into the eyes of a primate and it's like looking into a misty mirror. Someone a little like you stares back.

It's not really surprising. Primates – apes and monkeys – are our nearest relatives in the animal world. They fascinate us with their intelligence. They impress us with their agility. Some of them frighten us with their fearsome strength. Most of all, though, they remind us that we share the same forest-living, branch-swinging, fruit-eating ancestors.

MALE AND FEMALE
GIBBONS PAIR OFF
IN LIFELONG
RELATIONSHIPS.

APES
AND OTHER HAIRY PRIMATES

By
Richard Platt

Consultant
David Burnie

A Dorling Kindersley Book

Dorling **DK** Kindersley
LONDON, NEW YORK, SYDNEY, DELHI,
PARIS, MUNICH, and JOHANNESBURG

Project Editor Emma Johnson
Project Art Editor James Marks
Senior Editor Fran Jones
Senior Art Editor Marcus James
Category Publisher Jayne Parsons
Managing Art Editor Jacquie Gulliver
US Editors Gary Werner and Margaret Parrish
Picture Researcher Jo Haddon
Production Erica Rosen
DTP Designers Matthew Ibbotson and Louise Paddick

First American Edition 2001

01 02 03 04 05 10 9 8 7 6 5 4 3 2 1

Published in the United States by
DK Publishing, Inc.
95 Madison Avenue
New York, New York, 10016

A cataloging-in-publication record for this title is available from the Library of Congress

ISBN 0-7894-8003-4 (hc)
ISBN 0-7894-8019-0 (pb)

Reproduced by Colourscan, Singapore
Printed and bound by L.E.G.O., Italy

See our complete catalog at
www.dk.com

CONTENTS

INTRODUCTION

Coming face to face with a monkey or an ape is an experience you won't easily forget. In a forest clearing, in a wildlife park or zoo, even on film or TV – it doesn't matter where. Stare into the eyes of a primate and it's like looking into a misty mirror. Someone a little like you stares back.

It's not really surprising. Primates – apes and monkeys – are our nearest relatives in the animal world. They fascinate us with their intelligence. They impress us with their agility. Some of them frighten us with their fearsome strength. Most of all, though, they remind us that we share the same forest-living, branch-swinging, fruit-eating ancestors.

MALE AND FEMALE GIBBONS PAIR OFF IN LIFELONG RELATIONSHIPS.

This is a book about primates and their vanishing world. It begins with a look at all primates, and introduces the two most familiar kinds – apes and monkeys. Read on and you'll find out how they live in the wild, how they fight, and how they feed. You'll see how they get around in trees and on the ground; and how

WITH GRINS, FROWNS, AND HAND SIGNALS, CHIMPS HOLD LIVELY CONVERSATIONS.

they breed and raise their families. Then you'll learn about the many ways in which primates are similar to humans, and how scientists are trying to learn more about them.

We humans love our primate cousins. We admire them, too. But through greed and hunger we are destroying their forest homes and endangering their survival. So, at the end of the book there's a chapter on the threats to primates – and especially apes – with information about what you can do to help protect these intelligent creatures.

For those of you who want to explore the subject in more detail, there are black "Log On" boxes that appear throughout the book. These will direct you to some great websites where you can find out even more about the world of primates.

OUR APE ANCESTORS

T hey've got faces like ours. They've got hands like yours and mine. They can walk on two feet as we do.

PRIMATE HANDS ALL HAVE OPPOSABLE THUMBS LIKE OURS.

They're smart. And yet …apes and monkeys are not quite human. It's easy to see that we're alike in many ways. Scientists, who like neat names for groups of similar animals, call us all primates. But what are the features that put us in this group of primates, and who are our hairy relatives?

S hared features

Can you imagine having eyes where your ears are? Insects, birds, and some mammals (for example, horses) are built like this, but not primates. Having a pair of eyes on the front of a flat face is very useful. It allows us, as primates, to see in three dimensions, and to judge distances accurately.

Ape hands are the same as ours – four fingers and a thumb, whereas most other

APES HAVE A LONG CHILDHOOD – CHIMP KIDS RELY ON MOM FOR MORE THAN FIVE YEARS.

mammals have paws or hooves. Hands are handy for picking things up, and the thumb is especially useful. Primates all have opposable thumbs – they move in a different direction to the fingers, giving us a powerful grip. We primates have fingernails too, while other mammals have claws. And there are two less obvious differences. For one thing we're brainy. Even a stupid monkey learns quickly, and chimps are as smart in some ways as two-year-old children. The other difference is childhood. Most baby mammals have a tough time – their parents kick them out as soon as they can. But like human kids, baby monkeys and apes rely on mom and dad for longer.

The first primates

Scientists suggest that primates are alike because we all share the same ancestors. They explain the special abilities that primates share something like this. Mammals first appeared on Earth some 200 million

APES NEED SHARP EYES FOR FOREST LIFE

years ago. Those that lived in the forest learned to make the most of their surroundings. For example, mammals that could grip tree branches in their paws had an advantage over those that slipped from their leafy perches. The grippers got more food than the slippers and had more children. Gripper kids became even better at gripping – so their ability to hold

THE ABILITY TO GRIP BRANCHES MADE PRIMATES, SUCH AS THIS ORANGUTAN, SOME OF THE MOST SUCCESSFUL FOREST ANIMALS.

As evolution continued, the primate "family tree" branched out, and the various kinds of primates that we know today grew gradually more different. The first hominids (humanlike apes) appeared some seven million years ago. After that, hominids evolved into humans, apes got more apey, and monkeys became more monkeylike. So although chimpanzees are our relatives, they're very distant cousins indeed.

Most scientists agree that evolution explains why primates have similar features, but they can't *prove* that it's true. Some people don't accept that humans and apes share the same ancestors. They

improved with each generation. This process of development and slow improvement through breeding is called evolution. The first primates evolved about 65 million years ago.

P rimate evolution

All this doesn't mean that your great-great grandpa was a baboon with a big, blue butt.

SKELETONS FOUND AT TANZANIA'S OLDUVAI GORGE HELPED PROVE APES AND HUMANS SHARE ANCESTORS.

believe that God created humans and each kind of animal separately.

Primates alone would have kept God busy for a long while. There are 230 different species (unique types) of primates. Scientists divide this rich variety into three main groups – prosimians, monkeys, and apes.

LOG ON...
www.ucmp.berkeley.edu/history/evolution.html

The prosimians

The name prosimian means "before apes." It's a good description, because the prosimians have the most in common with the original prehistoric tree-swingers from which all primates descended.

By far the biggest group of prosimians, the lemurs, live on the giant island of Madagascar, off Africa's east coast. They lead mainly solitary lives and are most active at night. Lemurs' large eyes help them grab every scarce ray of light. Prosimians are small, and the

ALL THAT'S LEFT OF AUSTRALOPITHECUS, THE AFRICAN ANCESTOR OF ALL HUMANS.

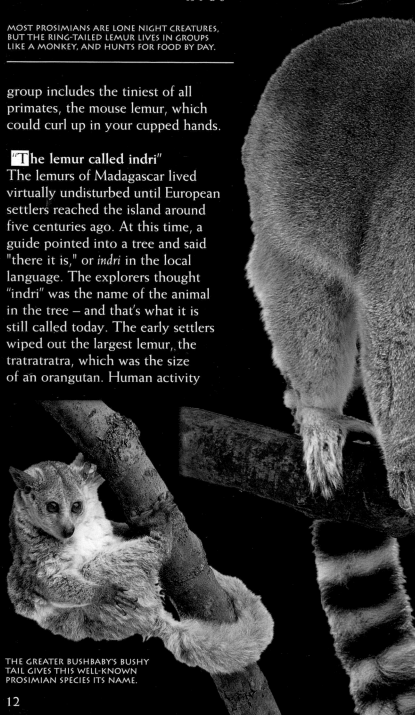

MOST PROSIMIANS ARE LONE NIGHT CREATURES,
BUT THE RING-TAILED LEMUR LIVES IN GROUPS
LIKE A MONKEY, AND HUNTS FOR FOOD BY DAY.

group includes the tiniest of all
primates, the mouse lemur, which
could curl up in your cupped hands.

"The lemur called indri"

The lemurs of Madagascar lived
virtually undisturbed until European
settlers reached the island around
five centuries ago. At this time, a
guide pointed into a tree and said
"there it is," or *indri* in the local
language. The explorers thought
"indri" was the name of the animal
in the tree – and that's what it is
still called today. The early settlers
wiped out the largest lemur, the
tratratratra, which was the size
of an orangutan. Human activity

THE GREATER BUSHBABY'S BUSHY
TAIL GIVES THIS WELL-KNOWN
PROSIMIAN SPECIES ITS NAME.

on Madagascar still
endangers rare lemurs.

The monkeys

On the primate scale, monkeys fall
between prosimians and apes. They are
smaller than apes, and not as smart; and
they also usually have tails (which apes
don't). Scientists separate them into New
World monkeys that live in forests in the

MARMOSETS ARE AMONG THE SMALLEST OF THE
MONKEYS. THIS SILVERY MARMOSET IS ABOUT
THE SIZE OF A SMALL RABBIT.

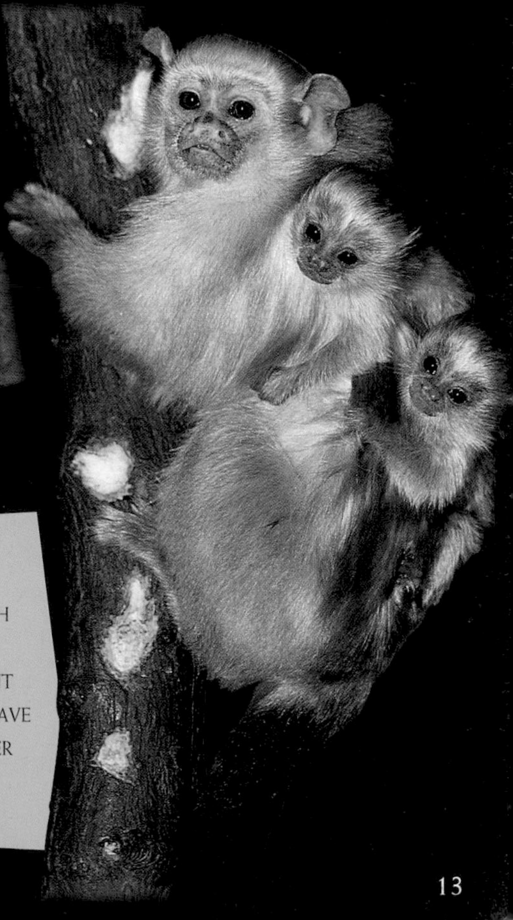

WEIRD WORLD

PROSIMIANS COMMUNICATE WITH
SMELLS. THEY HAVE SUPER-
SENSITIVE NOSES AND USE SCENT
GLANDS ON THEIR BODIES TO LEAVE
SMELLY MESSAGES THAT LINGER
FOR A WEEK OR MORE.

Americas, and Old World monkeys, which includes all the rest. Apart from their addresses, it's hard to tell Old and New World monkeys apart.

The apes

At the other end of the scale from the prosimians are the apes, a group to which we humans belong. There are only a few other species of ape – gibbons (which come in nine varieties), the great tree-dwelling orangutan of southeast Asia, and three African apes – the gorilla, chimpanzee, and the bonobo, or pygmy chimpanzee.

Humans

Although they are the most successful of the apes, humans (Homo sapiens) have an unusual disadvantage – they are almost hairless. They compensate for this by covering themselves with layers of clothes. Humans are to be found almost everywhere in the world, usually

SPIDER MONKEYS' TAILS ARE SO STRONG AND FLEXIBLE THAT THEY'RE AS USEFUL AS AN EXTRA LEG.

14

IN THE 1933 MOVIE KING KONG A GIANT
APE STALKED NEW YORK. ANIMATION
BROUGHT THE PUPPET APE TO LIFE.

living in "cities" – huge colonies of families. Despite their intelligence, humans are destructive. By competing for scarce resources, they are causing the extinction of many other animals.

Ape King

Apes seem so similar to humans that story tellers often use them to represent the animal urges that humans feel. King Kong is the most famous of these fictional apes. Real-life apes would never grow as big as King Kong, but some

CARTOONISTS DREW
DARWIN AS AN APE TO
MAKE FUN OF HIS IDEAS.

extinct apes were far bigger than those alive today. *Gigantopithecus*, which died out 5 million years ago, weighed about 660 lb (300 kg).

So, are we related or not?

Charles Darwin first proposed his theory of evolution in 1859. The next year biologist Thomas Huxley defended it against attack by Bishop Wilberforce, who asked whether Huxley had apes among his parent's ancestors. Today his jokes aren't so funny. The more we learn about the origins of human life, the more similarities we can find between humans and apes.

WHAT IS AN APE?

Think "ape" and you probably imagine scary, hairy, jungle giants swinging by their tails in the treetops ready to pounce on unsuspecting explorers. It makes a great story, but the truth is very different. For a start, apes don't have tails, and almost never attack people. In fact it's apes who are threatened by humans, not the other way around. The biggest ape – the gorilla – is a gentle vegetarian that lives on the ground.

Gorilla thriller

The king of the apes and the African forests is the gorilla. Gorillas are big! An adult male in the wild can grow to 610 lb (275 kg) – three or four times heavier than a man. Because of their size, a charging, chest-thumping angry gorilla is terrifying; but left alone, these apes are peaceful and harmless. They are mostly vegetarian, eating fruits, roots, and leaves, although

WEIRD WORLD
GORILLAS TALK IN GRUNTS, HOOTS, AND BELCHES. SCIENTISTS GAIN THEIR TRUST BY IMITATING THESE CALLS, SCRATCHING, AND SOMETIMES EVEN BEATING THEIR OWN CHESTS.

they may snack on the odd
creepy crawly. And though
they run at intruders, beating
their chests and snorting,
they usually back off.
Despite the Hollywood
image of a giant
tree-swinging
ape, the weight of
gorillas makes them
clumsy climbers. They live
mostly on the ground, walking
on their feet and knuckles.
They rarely stand upright.

A gorilla family is led by one
or two "silverbacks." These are
adult males, named after the
gray hair running across the
spine. Silverbacks jealously
guard their "wives" from
other affectionate
adult males.

However, the group may
include immature male gorillas,
who are no threat, as well as
females and their young.

GORILLA GROUPS
SPEND THE DAY
ON THE GROUND,
FEEDING, RESTING,
AND PLAYING.

There are three kinds of gorilla. The western lowland has a different shaped nose from the two that live farther east. You can tell these apart because the mountain version (thought by some to be a separate species) has a softer coat than the eastern lowland gorilla.

Chimp behavior

Gorillas may be the biggest of the apes, but if you are picking teams for a primate knowledge game show, choose a chimp any day. Chimpanzees are the closest animal relatives to the human race. They do lots of things we once thought only people did – such as learning languages and using tools. This doesn't mean they'll grab the toolbox and put up shelves or fix the car, but it does put them way ahead of other ape species in the smartness category.

Like gorillas, chimpanzees are Africans. You'll find them in most west and central forests, outside of the Congo

CHIMP ALLIANCES DEPEND ON HOW SCARCE FOOD IS. CHIMPANZEES WHO ARE BEST OF FRIENDS WHEN THEIR STOMACHS ARE FULL MAY FIGHT WHEN HUNGRY.

LOG ON..
www.enchantedlearning.com/subjects/apes

River basin. If chimps were human, you'd say they were tribal. They live in large groups of about 50 animals, though some chimp tribes are twice that size. In some areas the males patrol their territory, driving out or even killing other males that don't belong. Within the area of forest they control, chimp groups travel

As well as being smart, chimps are strong and powerful. A female chimp can lift a man with one hand.

Lightweight chimps
If chimp life is lively, then for bonobos, or pygmy

CHIMPS DRUM AND HOOT TO CALL THEIR FRIENDS TO RIPE FRUIT TREES

long distances in search of food, but they split up into smaller groups to hunt. They prefer fruit, but are not picky eaters. They will happily eat nuts, leaves, seeds, and insects – and meat. Chimpanzees sometimes organize hunting parties to track and kill colobus monkeys for food.

Because of their intelligence and large communities, chimps have a rich social life. When they are not gathering or eating food, or sleeping, they're busy grooming, playing, or mating.

chimpanzees, it's a party.
Food is plentiful in central Congo where these rare apes live, so they go collecting in

BONOBOS ARE UNIQUE AMONG APES BECAUSE MATURE FEMALES LIKE THIS ONE CONTROL THEIR GROUPS.

large groups. Sharing this experience makes bonobo life fun. Bonobos are also the most sexually active of all apes. Unusually, bonobos are feminists. That is to say, females lead the groups, and keep the males in line.

AN ADULT MALE ORANGUTAN HAS LARGE FATTY FLAPS ON EACH SIDE OF ITS FACE.

Despite the pygmy in their name, bonobos are no dwarfs. As tall as ordinary chimps, they are slightly lighter in weight and more agile. Because of these differences, they spend more time in the trees than regular chimps.

The orangutans

The African apes are sometimes called "great apes" because of their size and humanlike appearance. The only other great ape is the orangutan of Southeast Asia. Its name means "forest person" in the Malay language, and it's easy to see why. Reddish fur makes this ape very easy to recognize, but you'll be lucky to get the chance.

Hunting and logging of their rain forest home has driven orangutans close to extinction. Scarce food forces these apes to live lonely lives. When the forest bursts with fruit – maybe every five years – orangutans may gather for a dinner party. The rest of the time, males live alone, while females have their young to keep them company.

Orangutans are the largest tree-dwelling apes. At 200 lb (90 kg),

THE GIBBONS' SMALL SIZE AND AGILITY
ENABLE THEM TO CLIMB ON HIGH SLENDER
BRANCHES THAT LARGER APES WOULD
ALMOST CERTAINLY BREAK.

an adult male weighs more than a man. Too big to cross small branches, the ape must climb down the trunk to walk from tree to tree on feet and fists.

Females, which are half the weight of males, rarely come down to ground level.

Orangutans are quiet, peaceful animals – except for the males' "here-I-am" roars, they just smack their lips and grunt a little. Adults move slowly and deliberately – though young orangutans seem as full of energy as any human toddler.

The gibbons

Asia's other apes are the gibbons – there are some nine different kinds, living all over Southeast Asia's forests. The leaf-eating siamang is the largest species. The other, smaller gibbons feed mostly on fruit. Gibbons are the acrobats of the ape world, using their long arms to swing athletically from branch to branch. On the ground they look more awkward, walking upright with hands held high, or behind their backs.

Unlike most other mammals, gibbons are monogamous – males and females live in pairs, like a human husband and wife. Together they stake a claim to an area of forest and advertise their ownership with haunting "duets." The song may not be very musical to human ears, but it helps keep the pair together and fends off rivals.

21

MONKEY GALLERY

How can you tell the difference between Old World and New World monkeys? Simple. Old World monkeys live in the so-called "Old World" – Africa and Asia – while New World monkeys hang out in Central and South America. To make sure, look at their noses and tails. New World monkeys have wider, sideways-pointing nostrils, and most have prehensile tails for gripping branches. Still confused? Ask a dentist. New World monkeys have four extra teeth.

All present and correct
Scientists have divided monkeys into so many different families, groups, species, and races that the whole business of naming and classifying looks quite bewildering to non-experts. So here's a quick rundown of monkeys, starting with the Old World.

Old World monkeys
Leaf-eating monkeys (colobines) of Africa and Asia have noticeable pot bellies. They don't get this like a human would, by sitting in front of a TV eating chips. The colobines' pear-shaped figure comes from its diet. These monkeys need double stomachs and long digestive systems to digest their bulky food.

Africa's colobines are the colobus

THESE LIVELY MONA MONKEYS LIVE IN THE FORESTS OF WEST AFRICA. THEY LEAP THROUGH THE TREES, FEEDING ON LEAVES, FRUITS, AND INSECTS.

monkeys. Black-and-white colobus have beautiful coats and were once hunted for fur. All colobus monkeys are becoming rarer, and red colobus are endangered. There are more colobines – nearly 30 different kinds – in Asia. The long-haired langurs are found all the way from India to the Southeast Asian islands. Thanks to their tree-based diet and

even lives in towns. (It's named after the Hindu monkey god, Hanuman.)

Asian colobines also include Borneo's extraordinary proboscis monkey, named for the male's dangly nose. The proboscis monkey has another unusual characteristic – it's a strong swimmer and will even dive underwater to avoid capture.

lifestyle they are good leapers, although a few langurs have adapted to life out of the trees. The large Hanuman langur, India's sacred temple monkey,

THE PURPOSE OF THE PROBOSCIS MONKEY'S CURIOUS DANGLING NOSE IS A MYSTERY. SCIENTISTS CAN'T EXPLAIN HOW OR WHY IT EVOLVED.

WEIRD WORLD
TAME TEMPLE MONKEYS ARE CONSIDERED SO SACRED THAT THOSE KILLED IN ACCIDENTS GET A FULL HINDU FUNERAL.

B ig baboons

Other Old World monkeys choose their meals from a bigger menu. Baboons, the largest African monkeys, have even been known to hunt and kill antelope for food. The baboon's "anything goes" attitude to meals has made them a very successful breed. You'll find them in many different African environments, from forest to near-desert.

Baboons have had to adapt to life on the ground to survive in these very different homes. Gelada baboons, which live in the Ethiopian highlands, take this to the limit. They are so used to life on the ground that they can't climb and probably wouldn't recognize a tree if one fell on them.

V ersatile macaques

Baboons may be Africa's most widely distributed monkeys, but macaques have made adaptability an art form. No other primate – except for humans – is so widespread. You'll find macaques in frosty northern Japan and all the way across Asia to northwest Africa's Atlas Mountains. They're even in Europe – the Barbary "apes" of Gibraltar, on Spain's bottom right corner, are a kind of macaque.

BABOONS' RAZOR-SHARP TEETH ENABLE THEM TO CARVE UP GAME THEY HUNT DOWN. HERE, THEY'RE EATING ANTELOPE.

ADAPTABLE MACAQUES IN JAPAN COMBAT THE FROSTY CLIMATE BY TAKING A BATH IN A HOT SPRING.

won't mistake them for any other monkey. Big and short-tailed, they look like they've gone crazy with the stage greasepaint. Mandrills have red, white, and blue on their faces and sex organs, and brilliantly colored butts. Black-faced drills share the mandrill's garish behind. Both feed on the ground, but sleep in trees.

F unny guenons

Africa's other monkeys are the graceful, slim guenons. There are about 24 different kinds,

SMART MONKEYS RAID CROPS WHEN WILD FOOD RUNS OUT

Why do macaques do so well, when other monkey populations are declining? Because they've learned to get along well with humans. Too well, perhaps. In some urban areas, macaques have become destructive pests.

C olorful characters

Drills and mandrills are closely related to baboons, but are found only in the densest forests of West Africa. You and the patas and vervet are the most widespread. They range almost everywhere south of the Sahara, through the equatorial rain forests to the deserts and plains of southern Africa. Like baboons, they owe their success to their ability to live on the ground. Other guenons are tree-dwellers, and they are found in smaller pockets of jungle and forest.

Many guenons are beautiful to look at. Their dense, soft fur

THE WORLD'S SMALLEST MONKEY, THE PYGMY MARMOSET, IS ABOUT THREE TIMES THE SIZE OF A MOUSE.

squirrels in size and movement. Unusually for primates, they have claws to help them climb. The main difference between them is their teeth. A marmoset's chisel-shaped jaw can bite into tree bark and drink the gum that flows out of it. Tamarins generally prefer insects and fruit.

is marked with white or bright colors in patterns that enable us to tell them apart.

New World monkeys

These monkeys are all forest-dwellers. The smallest, the tamarins and the marmosets, divide up their Amazon home as ruthlessly as street gangs. North and west of the Amazon and Madeira rivers, the tamarins are bosses. South and east? Hey! That's a marmoset neighborhood.

Apart from their homes, there's not much difference between them. Both types of monkey are small, a little like

What else is on the menu? Larger New World monkeys dine on fruits, leaves, and seeds. The seed specialists are the saki and uakari monkeys. In the dry season nuts and seeds make up more than three-quarters of the saki's diet. Some even have specially adapted mouths so that they can crack open the hardest nuts with their teeth. Don't try this yourself!

There are three species of uakaris, and two of them have extraordinary bald faces. The bald uakari is also called the English monkey, because its red

WEIRD WORLD

JUST AS SOME HUMANS MARK THEIR PLACE AT THE TABLE WITH PERSONALIZED NAPKIN RINGS, MARMOSETS "CLAIM" A HOLE IN TREE BARK BY PEEING ON IT WHEN THEY FINISH DRINKING THE SAP.

LOG ON…
www.mc.maricopa.edu/
academic/cult_sci/anthro/
primates/new_monkeys.html

THE HOWLER MONKEY'S LOUD CALL FILLS
THE AMAZON FOREST EACH MORNING.

face and white body makes it look like an Englishman who has spent too long in the sun. Uakaris are not as nuts about nuts as the sakis, and eat fruit and leaves as well as seeds.

Noisy leaf eaters

The New World's leaf eaters are the howler monkeys. They are famous not for their diet, but for their voices – howlers are the world's noisiest land animal (only whales have louder voices). They yell out their ownership of a forest corner with a cry that carries up to 10 miles (16 km). A shell-like bone under the chin acts like an echo chamber to amplify the call. To digest tough leaves, they are lucky to have very strong digestive systems – leaves ferment in their lower intestines.

Fruit eaters

The other American monkeys are mostly fruit eaters, though

27

monkeys and are named for the hairy crests on their heads, which make them look like monks of the Capuchin order.

Squirrel monkeys eat insects and spiders to add protein to their fruity diet. These small monkeys look for food in large groups – sometimes as many as 500-strong. Banding together like this provides protection against their larger animal enemies.

Night monkeys have a different way of avoiding being someone else's lunch. True to

OWL OR NIGHT MONKEYS ARE NOT AS WELL ADAPTED TO THE DARK AS PROSIMIANS – THEY PREFER TO HUNT BY BRIGHT MOONLIGHT.

DEFORESTATION THREATENS MONKEYS WORLDWIDE

they are not strict about this. There's not much protein in fruit, so they all eat other things to get a balanced diet. Capuchins are the least particular of all, and will eat snails, insects, and small creatures. Their varied diet has allowed them to spread almost everywhere in the South American rain forests. Capuchins are the smartest of the New World

THE CAPUCHIN MONKEY'S INTELLIGENCE MAKES IT EASY TO TAME – MANY ARE TRAPPED FOR SALE AS PETS.

28

SQUIRREL MONKEYS KEEP UP A CONTINUOUS CHATTER OF PEEPS, TWITTERS, AND CLUCKS TO KEEP IN TOUCH WITH THEIR COMPANIONS.

their name, they wake up when the sun sets. Though this is common among prosimians, night monkeys are special – no other family of monkeys is nocturnal.

Titi monkeys are a little bigger than squirrel monkeys, but they don't look for food in the same large groups. Mom, dad, and kids gather fruit together, throwing in leaves or insects for additional protein.

Finally, spider monkeys are the biggest of the New World monkeys. Their long arms and flexible shoulders make them agile acrobats in the trees. They swing along with help from their prehensile tails, which are strong enough to support their weight. Bands of spider monkeys forage together high in the trees – they hardly ever come down to ground level.

Mega-monkeys!

You've probably guessed that there are a lot of monkeys out there. They may not be quite as "humanlike" as the apes, but their large numbers make them easier to find in the wild, and the sheer variety of their lifestyles and behavior make them just as interesting as their bigger, brighter ape cousins.

29

NOT SO CUDDLY

Apes' smiles and monkeys' pranks may make them hard to resist. However, primates are not cuddly toys – they are wild animals of the forest. Some are strong enough to tear your arm off. Others fight and kill to survive – when a predator pounces, the best defense is often to attack. Primates also use fighting and killing in other ways. For instance, violence helps them get the food they need and ensures that the strongest and fittest get the most chances to find a partner and have big healthy babies.

Fighting for life

In the forest monkeys don't often have to fight for their lives, because there are usually safer ways to avoid becoming "dish of the day" for a stalking predator. For example, when an eagle soars over Amazonia, monkeys beneath scatter into the densest parts of the forest, safe from the eagle's sharp talons. However, primates that live on the ground run more of a risk of being caught – and this danger has made baboons into the street-fighting gangs of the primate world.

A baboon has powerful jaws that operate like a knife and grindstone to keep the front teeth razor sharp. It's a foolish jackal that will tackle a male baboon on its own.

To protect their females and young, baboons mount guards. The strongest males act as "sentries," often sitting on tall termite mounds to keep watch. When danger threatens, the males may gang up to fight, or at least frighten, the intruder. Their ferocious bites are enough to fend off all but the most powerful attackers.

A CHIMP'S BARED TEETH AND WIDE MOUTH CLEARLY SAY "I AM ANGRY!"

RATHER THAN FIGHT A LEOPARD, MONKEYS TRY TO ESCAPE. IT'S AN UNEVEN RACE, THOUGH, BECAUSE LEOPARDS ARE FASTER AND MAY EVEN CLIMB TREES.

Fighting and loving

The baboons' fierce and threatening dental equipment did not evolve to defend them against all predators. For in the baboon world, if you want to find a mate, you have to fight for it, and big, sharp teeth are a definite advantage.

Baboon society is a little like an old-fashioned royal garden party. At the palace, the guests

WEIRD WORLD
PRIMATES MAY PAY A HIGH PRICE FOR BOSSINESS. DOMINANT OLIVE BABOONS HAVE FEWER BABIES THAN THOSE THEY BULLY – PERHAPS BECAUSE IT'S "TOUGH AT THE TOP" AND STRESS MAKES THEM LESS FERTILE.

line up in a strict order, according to the importance of their family. It's the same among male baboons, except that aggression, not birth, decides your place in the line-up. The biggest, meanest, toothiest baboon at the head of the line is called the alpha male. For baboons there's more at stake than who gets first crack at the snacks. The prize for the alpha male's aggression is the prettiest, most fertile females. But not all primates fight to decide which guy gets the girl. Even among those that do, actual fights are

NOISY CALLING MARKS PRIMATE TERRITORY ALMOST AS WELL AS FIGHTING.

LOG ON...
www.gorilla-haven.
org/ghetiquette.htm

AN ALPHA MALE IN A BABOON TROOP SHOWS HIS RIVALS WHAT THEY FACE IF THEY WANT TO CHALLENGE HIS POWER.

can feed their young. How much fighting there is depends on the food supply. In hungry times, fur flies as the girls battle over who gets what. But when there's plenty of food around, female vervets are the best of friends again.

Hunting parties

Chimpanzees put their aggression to good use when food is in short supply, by organizing hunting parties. Chimps are mainly vegetarian, but turn to meat in the dry season when they can't find enough fruits, seeds, berries, and leaves. They hunt small bushbuck or colobus monkeys. Chimp hunts are cooperative

rare and short. Much more common are threats of violence, which take the form of "I am the greatest" face-making contests of bared teeth and low growls.

CHIMPS DON'T JUST EAT MEAT – THEY KILL AND EAT EACH OTHER

Female fighters

Aggression isn't just a guy thing. In many primate species, such as vervet monkeys, females compete violently, too. For them, though, the ultimate prize is food. The more food they can get a hold of, the better they

affairs in which males that don't usually have much to do with each other get together to surround a colobus, then close in for the kill.

Chimp hunts can take a murderous turn if there's a chance of grabbing territory from a neighboring group.

BABOON BITES CAUSE SERIOUS WOUNDS, BUT LUCKILY MOST BATTLES ARE MORE LIKE ANGRY DANCES THAN REAL FIGHTS.

Territory fights are common throughout the natural world, wherever animals compete for a limited amount of space. Primates fight for space just like other animals, but sometimes chimpanzees take violence to the limit – they are the only primates we know of that deliberately kill off rivals in neighboring groups. In a grisly cannibalistic twist, they sometimes tear apart and eat the bodies of their victims.

The strength of an ape

In spite of their size, chimps are as musclebound as any human bodybuilder. To give you some idea of their strength, a female chimp can lift a man (or woman) with just one of her hands.

Gorillas are so much larger than chimps that their strength is obvious for all to see – would you challenge a gorilla to an arm-wrestling contest? In fact, gorillas in the wild are gentle animals that usually pose no danger to humans. They attack only when they are threatened. But when they do, watch out! In 1999, Max, a gorilla at Johannesburg Zoo in South Africa, was shot and wounded by a criminal who jumped into his cage. When two police officers jumped in and chased the gunman, the enraged gorilla picked up one cop under each long arm.

THE GORILLA'S HUGE SIZE AND FRIGHTENING SNARL HAVE GIVEN IT A FIERCE REPUTATION IT DOESN'T DESERVE.

WEIRD WORLD
GORILLAS THAT MAKE CHEST-
BEATING RUSHES AT HUMANS ARE
USUALLY LARGE SILVERBACKS. THE
AIM OF THESE TANTRUMS IS TO
PROTECT THEIR CLAN OF FEMALES
AND YOUNGER MALES.

EATING OUT

I f primates ate in restaurants, what would they choose from the menu? A hungry baboon might pick a juicy antelope steak, but fruit cocktail would be dish of the day – every day – because fruits are a favorite of most monkeys and apes. There would be orders for nut cutlet and tossed salad, and tree gum cup would appeal to marmosets. The full menu would also include side orders of beetles, ants, mushrooms, and honey.

Available food

How do we know what apes and monkeys eat? Of course, we can watch them and keep a careful record of the foods they choose, but with shy animals this is difficult or impossible. Fortunately, there is another way to go. Everything that goes in one end comes out the other, so by studying droppings in microscopic detail, scientists learn a lot about primate diet.

BESIDES THE WILD CELERY THIS SILVERBACK IS EATING, GORILLAS ALSO ENJOY ANTS, NETTLES, BAMBOO, THISTLES, AND FRUIT.

Eating what's available

A few primates are custom-built for eating certain kinds of food. Good examples are the nut-cracker teeth of the saki, and the long, churning, fermenting intestines of some leaf-eating monkeys. However, even these primates can't afford to be picky eaters, because the forest is not like a well-stocked supermarket. If their favorite food is hard to find apes have to switch to something that's more plentiful.

PRIMATES ARE MESSY EATERS. THEY TASTE EVERYTHING, AND SPIT OUT UNRIPE FRUIT.

This ability to switch has made primatologists (scientists who study primates) cautious about calling one monkey or ape a fruit eater and another a seed eater. While this may be true at one place in the forest, not too far away the same species may have a different diet. Highland gorillas, for instance, eat a lot of leaves, but Western Lowland gorillas include more fruit in their diet.

THE RAMBUTAN FRUIT WOULD MAKE A TASTY DESSERT FOR MALAYSIA'S RARE ORANGUTAN.

Eat while ripe

Most primates love fruit, and it's a good thing they do. Fruit seeds pass unchanged through the intestines of the animal that ate them. The seeds emerge in a pellet of manure, far from the tree where the fruit was picked. It's a neat arrangement – the primate gets a meal and the seeds get free transportation.

Trees that rely on animals to spread their seeds in this way make their fruits tempting and tasty – but not until the seeds are ready for sowing. Until then the fruit may be offensive: hard, the wrong color, and bitter with chemicals called tannins.

37

If you've ever picked and eaten an apple before it's ready you'll know the feeling.

All primates prefer ripe fruit. Indeed for apes — and humans — fruit has to be ripe to be digested. Unripe fruit can do more than just make us say "yuck." It can give us an upset stomach. However, it's a different story with monkeys. They prefer ripe fruit, but can digest unripe fruit if necessary.

Apes and monkeys find it easy to recognize ripe fruits, checking and rejecting those that aren't ready with a sniff or a quick bite.

THE COLOBUS MONKEY DIGESTS LEAVES IN A DOUBLE STOMACH — MUCH LIKE A COW WITH FOUR STOMACHS DIGESTS GRASS.

T wo for the price of one
Unlike fruit, leaves are not the most popular choice for apes and monkeys, because they don't contain much food. They are made mainly of a fiber, for other primates — few pig out on leaves.

Colobine monkeys — colobus monkeys and langurs — are the exception. They eat

MONKEYS CAN EAT – AND THRIVE – ON UNRIPE FRUIT

called cellulose, which is unaffected by the acids and chemicals found in the intestines of primates — humans included. You may enjoy a green salad for lunch, but it will pass through you pretty much undigested. It's the same story little else but leaves. They can do this because they have evolved an ingenious solution to the digestion problem. Instead of one stomach, they have two! Bacteria (simple microscopic bugs) in the upper stomach break down the fiber and release energy from it. The acid-filled lower stomach is more like our own. For colobines digestion is a slow process, so they spend a lot of time chilling out.

The howler monkeys of the South American forests also live mainly on leaves, but their stomachs, though large, are more ordinary. To aid digestion they grind the leaves up very finely before swallowing.

Just because these monkeys eat leaves, it doesn't mean that they eat just any leaves. Some trees have poisonous foliage.

Even in trees with edible leaves, the new shoots are the most succulent and tasty.

Nutcracker

Primates that eat seeds face a different problem, because many plants protect their seeds specifically to stop animals from eating them. Scientists call the woody outer layer of these seeds endocarps, but you or I would say "nuts."

A few primates have jaws like nutcrackers, especially the bearded saki, which can even crack hard Brazil nuts. Other monkeys find opening hard nuts a frustrating business.

CHIMPS ARE GREAT AT USING TOOLS. THEY CRACK NUTS WITH SPECIALLY SELECTED HAMMER STONES.

Grivet monkeys simply tap them together in the hope of breaking the shell. This works for thin-shelled nuts, but not for the tougher variety.

Chimpanzees are smarter. Some have learned to break open nuts using a hammer stone. The hardest nuts need a really heavy rock to crack the shell – a human adult would find it difficult to lift stones of this weight and bring them down with enough accuracy to crush the shell, but chimps are strong and can do it time and time again.

Meaty feast

Only a few primates are strong, smart, or agile enough to catch and eat mammals and birds. Baboons and chimps hunt smaller primates for food, and baboons also catch birds, hares, and young antelope. Though capuchins aren't such expert hunters, they will eat small mammals, such as mice, which are not fast enough to scamper to safety.

Many other primates eat meat, but not the fur and feather variety. Instead, hungry apes and monkeys snack on insects, moths, grubs, spiders, and lizards. These creepy-crawly mouthfuls are especially valuable to fruit-eating primates, because they are high

in protein, the essential growth food that most fruits lack.

Exotic eaters

Tucked away at the bottom of the menu at the Primate Bar & Grill are a few exotic specialties. Tree gum is the food of choice for prosimians such as lemurs and bushbabies, but the only gum-eating monkeys are the tamarins and marmosets. Their specially shaped front teeth enable them to bite through the tree bark to make the gum flow.

Flowers are another plant food that most larger primates tend to ignore, but tamarins and capuchins have been known to suck the sweet nectar from blossoms.

A CHIMP RETURNS FROM HUNTING WITH A MEATY MEAL. UNTIL THE 1960S, CHIMPS WERE THOUGHT TO BE VEGETARIANS.

Food affects behavior

Among monkeys the food supply makes the difference between a friendly feast and a fight. Monkeys live in large groups, and when there's plenty of food they may feed together peacefully. Hunger, though, causes feuds and aggression within the same group. Then the monkeys will fight to decide who eats first.

Apes' preference for ripe fruit forces them to live quite differently. Tropical forests don't have a spring-summer-fall-winter cycle, so there isn't a season for each particular fruit. Instead there is always ripe fruit somewhere in the forest – but where? If apes foraged for food in large groups, like monkeys, they would starve, because trees with ripe fruit are so far apart. Instead they look for food in small groups, or alone.

Leaf-eating primates tend not to be very competitive and aggressive, partly because their food is quite abundant, but also because they are too tired. Digesting leaves uses up a large amount of their energy, and they don't have much left for fighting over who should be leader of the pack.

WHEN THERE'S LOTS OF FOOD, CHIMPS CALL THEIR FRIENDS AND SHARE .

GETTING AROUND

To monkeys, humans must seem pitifully inadequate. Why do they wait at the side of busy roads when they could just swing from the streetlights, high above the traffic? They can't climb! The poor things need stairs to get up to the second floor of their houses! And how on earth do they manage without tails? It's true, we humans may have an advantage when it comes to walking upright, but in all other ways our primate cousins are better designed for getting around.

SOUTH AMERICA'S OWL MONKEY HARDLY HAS TO STRETCH TO REACH ACROSS A GAP THIS WIDE.

Swinging through trees
When we think of monkeys and apes moving around in the forest, we usually think of them climbing nimbly in trees. However, there's nimble and just nimble in the climbing department – some primates are better at it than others. And what we call climbing actually involves a lot of different skills. These include using both hands and legs to clamber from branch,

to branch; shinning up trees by gripping the trunk mainly with the legs, running along branches on all fours, and perhaps a little leaping around.

Going for gold
If there were primate Olympic games, each of these activities would be a separate event, and no one species would win them all. Most monkeys would compete in branch-walking on all fours – it's the most popular

MONKEYS ARE FAMOUS FOR CLIMBING TREE TRUNKS, BUT APES – LIKE THIS CHIMPANZEE – ARE BETTER AT SHINNING UP THE BARK.

Monkeys make poor trunk-climbers because their shoulders have limited movement – they find it difficult to stretch up and grab higher branches. Apes are better at climbing. They have longer arms and flatter chests than monkeys, and their more flexible shoulders give them a higher reach.

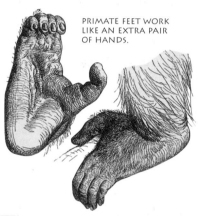

PRIMATE FEET WORK LIKE AN EXTRA PAIR OF HANDS.

way of getting around in the tree tops, and for primates with legs longer than arms, it's safe and efficient. Colobus monkeys, though, would win a gold for the leaping, because they have evolved powerful hind legs for daring jumps.

Get a grip

Primates' hands are wonderfully adapted to climbing, because they can grip branches with their fingers and thumbs. All primates, except for humans, have big toes that work like thumbs for clinging on. This might seem odd to you, but it wouldn't surprise Amazonian people who live in the forest. Some climb trees constantly, and by using their big toes to grip, have developed muscular feet more like those of a gorilla than a shoe-wearing human.

Tree swingers

What's white, sweet and fluffy,
and swings from tree to tree?
A meringue-utang! This terrible
old joke contains a core of
truth, for swinging really is a
piece of cake for orangutans.
However, their heavy weight
restricts them to the thicker
branches, and they actually
prefer walking and
climbing.

Many other primates can
swing by their hands, but few
are as good at it as gibbons,
siamangs, and spider monkeys.
They're all much lighter
than orangutans and
hurl themselves around
more nimbly than the
best human athletes.

ONLY YOUNG ORANGUTANS ARE
LIGHT ENOUGH TO SWING FROM
BRANCHES HIGH IN THE FOREST.

44

Hanging on

Gibbons can do this because through evolution their bodies have changed to help them swing. Their arms are very long compared to their legs, and their wrists are double-jointed so that they can turn in a full circle. This isn't literally true. Gibbons don't actually have two joints where other primates have one, but their wrists are flexible and loosely jointed

To see what this means, turn your own wrist. Start with the hand palm down, turn it palm up, and keep on turning. How much further can you turn it? A gibbon would keep going until it was palm down again.

Gibbons' shoulders are almost as flexible as their wrists.

If you see a gibbon in a zoo, watch it carefully as it swings, and think of circus performers. Trapeze artists in the big top use a rope or a swing to build up speed and propel themselves through the air. A gibbon doesn't need a swing, because its long arms give its agile to-and-fro action extra energy.

Walking on the ground

At last! An event in which humans stand a decent chance – but only if it's a two-legged

45

race. On four legs, some non-human primates, such as patas monkeys, can easily outrun an Olympic sprinter. Patas monkeys are fast runners because they spend most of their time on the ground, and have evolved (developed over time) legs and arms of roughly the same length. Other ground-dwelling primates have adapted in a similar way. However, the tree dwellers, with their longer legs, are more clumsy on the ground.

Great apes and monkeys walk in slightly different ways. The apes walk with their knuckles on the ground. Monkeys prefer a "palms-down" approach. A grassland lifestyle has given baboons a very special way of walking on all fours. They press their fingers on the ground, but with their palms raised. This lifts their heads, helping them to keep a wary eye open for any sign of danger in the distance.

Many of the primates

APES' HANDS HAVE A NATURAL CURVE, SO WHEN THEY WALK ON ALL FOURS, THEY PLACE THEIR KNUCKLES ON THE GROUND.

can manage a pace or two on the ground without using their hands. Gorillas, chimps, gibbons, spider monkeys, macaques, and capuchins all cope quite well on two

MONKEYS LIKE THIS GUENON WALK WITH PALMS DOWN.

legs. Humans, though, are specially adapted to standing upright and walking. We have long, powerful legs, a curved spine, and strong hips. Thanks to these advantages, humans are the only primates that can stride – walk easily with long steps at a flowing pace.

Tail piece

What we can't do, though, is hang upside down from a branch without using our arms and legs. But what's impossible for humans comes perfectly naturally to spider monkeys.

THE TAIL OF SOUTH AMERICA'S WOOLY MONKEY IS SO MUSCULAR AND SOLID THAT IT LOOKS LIKE A FIFTH LIMB.

MONKEYS CARRYING FOOD WALK EASILY ON THREE LEGS

They have prehensile (from Latin *prehendere* meaning "to grasp") tails – long, muscular extensions to the spine that are quite strong enough to support their whole weight. Though no other species of monkey uses its tail with quite the same skill, most other New World monkeys have long tails, and use them for gripping and balance. Now if you had a tail like a spider monkey, how would you make use of it when nobody was looking?

47

PRIMATE PARTNERS

Breeding and raising young are as important for primates as they are for other animals. Some pair off in a lifelong "marriage." But most primates raise several families with different partners. Finding just the right partner demands careful timing, skillful planning, and good grooming – fighting skills are an advantage, too!

Together forever

Gibbons are the most loyal of all primates. They "pair bond," or stick together, like a devoted wife and husband.

This monogomy is unusual anywhere in the mammal world, and among apes and monkeys it's almost unique.

It's puzzling, too, because sticking together like this does not seem to offer any real advantages. Males don't carry or feed the youngsters, and they don't even keep other gibbons away from the family food. By staying with just one female, males miss valuable opportunities to father baby gibbons with other females. Baffled scientists have tried to guess why. Perhaps male gibbons become loyal fathers as a way of protecting their children until they grow to adulthood.

It's about survival

Gibbons loyalty, though, is the exception. Most other apes and monkeys form partnerships that last just long enough to reproduce, and no longer. How they find their partners is fascinating and sometimes amusing. It often looks a

SWELLINGS ON THE RUMPS OF MANY FEMALE APES AND MONKEYS SIGNAL THAT THEY ARE READY TO BREED.

lot like human romance. Some apes play games that seem similar to teenage dating. And when romances go wrong there's trouble – and even violent flare-ups.

Whatever the approach, primate dating and mating has one simple goal – to make more monkeys and apes. To understand primate relationships it's useful to

MALE BABOONS COLLECT AS MANY WIVES AS THEY CAN DEFEND FROM RIVALS.

WEIRD WORLD
FEMALE PRIMATES ARE NOT FERTILE WHILE THEY ARE RAISING THEIR YOUNG. SO, IMPATIENT MALES SOMETIMES KILL THE CHILDREN FATHERED BY RIVALS – THEN MATE WITH THE MOTHER.

LIKE MALES, FEMALE BABOONS FIGHT TO BE "NUMBER ONE," BUT THEY BATTLE FOR THE BEST FOOD, NOT OVER MATING.

remember a few simple rules. Male primates want big families – and lots of them. So they need to have as many female children grow up is more important than simply having lots of babies.

A ttracting a mate

The routine of dating and mating depends on the

FOR MALES NUMBERS MATTER – THEY WANT LOTS OF KIDS

partners as they can. For females, things aren't quite so simple. They are more interested in quality than quantity, because their children will inherit both parent's best points (and their worst!) For a female, ensuring that her fertility of females, since most primates only mate when there is a chance of becoming pregnant. At these fertile times, the appearance of a female's body may change, giving a visual signal that attracts the opposite sex.

50

Other changes are less obvious – for example, fertile female monkeys may have a different scent. Their behavior changes, too. They encourage males in ways that sometimes seem flirtatious – long, lingering stares, or pretending not to be interested in a chosen partner.

Male behavior also changes when they are interested in a female. Instead of buying gifts, primates groom their chosen partner. This popular activity has special importance at breeding time. Grooming relieves stress, and this in turn boosts female fertility. So, by grooming his partner, a male primate not only relaxes her, he also increases the possibility that she will have his children.

BABOONS ARE AS PROUD AND PROTECTIVE OF THEIR YOUNG AS ANY HUMAN PARENT.

Rivals for affection
Among monkeys that live in small groups mating behavior is simplest – the strongest male can keep all his "wives" for himself, and fight off competitors. In baboon groups, for example, these battles to be the top male can be bloody and vicious, leaving a trail of bleeding bites and broken bones. Among monkeys that live in bigger groups, one male can't hope to keep track of all the fertile females, so several males share control.

Apes behave differently. Female apes are not fertile while they are breastfeeding their young, and this continues for several years. It makes life frustrating for male apes, who are eager to father more young. So that they don't miss a single opportunity, male apes figure out clever ways to make sure they are in the right part of the forest when a female is fertile.

Finding a mate

Gorillas make the mating game work for them by gathering together a harem of several females and driving off other males. For orangutans, this would be a dumb idea, because females forage (hunt for food) far and wide in the forest.

GROOMING IS AN IMPORTANT PART OF APE MATING. IT'S A "KISS AND A HUG" THAT ENCOURAGES SOMETHING MORE SERIOUS.

GROOMING MAKES FEMALES MORE RELAXED – AND MORE FERTILE

Orangutan males try to control the largest possible area, making sure that they have the pick of females within it.

Chimpanzee males have to be more adaptable, because female behavior depends on food supply. When there is plenty

A MALE ORANGUTAN'S TOOTHY WARNING KEEPS RIVALS AWAY FROM HIS MATE. HIS "FACE FLANGES" REINFORCE THE MESSAGE.

to eat, females collect food in groups, and it pays a male chimp to tag along in case one of the group is fertile. When food is scarce, this plan does not work, because female chimps can collect more by splitting up and foraging alone. Then a male stands more chance of mating if he behaves like an orangutan, defending part of the forest so that he can claim the females within it. In some regions, male chimps become very possessive about their neighborhood and the females in it. They form gangs and work together, guarding their section of the forest and driving off (or even killing) rivals that stray into it to try their luck with fertile females.

Deadly dads

Murderous competition for mates doesn't just affect outsiders. Because females are not fertile when they are feeding babies, a male ape or monkey sometimes kills the children of his rivals, so that he can mate with the mother. For example, in India, many groups of temple monkeys have a single male leader, who mates with all the females. If a rival male fights for and manages to win control of the group, he will try to kill all the young monkeys. He knows they are not his children and only by killing them will he be able to mate with the mothers and father children of his own.

Bottom line

So what about those extraordinary bulging lumps on their rumps? Many types of Old World monkeys develop these swellings, but they are at their most startling and flamboyant on mangabeys, baboons, and chimpanzees. When females are fertile, their butts increase in size like an inflated tire. Their rumps change color, too — sometimes to a bright red. It's such an

FAITHFUL GIBBONS PAIR OFF IN A MARRIAGE THAT LASTS A LIFETIME.

obvious invitation that a male monkey cannot help but notice.

Female geladas put an interesting twist on the big-pink-bulges routine – since they spend most of their time sitting down, the bright red swelling appears instead on their chests.

Male primates have a colorless sex life compared to females, with one exception – male vervet monkeys have sex organs decorated in shades of red, white, and powder blue. Dominant male vervets show off their power by circling less powerful males with this colorful part proudly on view. Primatologists have nicknamed this show "the red-white-and-blue display."

A GELADA'S CHEST SWELLING FORMS A BRIGHT PINK HOURGLASS PATTERN.

Growing up

Mating is the just the beginning of a long family story, since primate young depend on their parents for food and protection longer than the children of most other mammals. Gibbons, for instance, stay with their parents for up to eight years before they go off to find a mate and start their own family.

During their long childhood, monkeys and apes learn not only how to survive successfully without mom and dad, but also how to fit in to primate society and follow its set of rules.

WEIRD WORLD

APES HAVE A LONG CHILDHOOD, DURING WHICH THEY LEARN TO SURVIVE IN THE FOREST. SOME ARE NOT FULLY GROWN UNTIL THEY ARE ABOUT 10-15 YEARS OLD.

LIVING TOGETHER

I magine you are the only human being in the world. How would you find enough food? What would you do if wild beasts attacked? Could you keep yourself clean? It's easy to see the advantages of living in families and societies – bigger groups – where everyone helps each other out. It's the same for apes and monkeys. They form family groups, and most stick together in societies like our own.

BABY CHIMPS FEED ON MOTHER'S MILK UNTIL THEY ARE ABOUT FIVE YEARS OLD.

Almost human

Watching how primates behave in groups it's hard not to recognize the habits of our brothers, sisters, and friends. They talk, play, fight, share meals, keep each other clean, and some even make beds! No wonder we're tempted to shout "Look, they're almost human!" One of the reasons why primate society seems so similar to our own is that young apes and monkeys take a long time to grow up. The young of most mammals become independent within a year, often much less. Dogs are puppies for only eight months, lambs become sheep in a similar time, mice grow up in just five weeks. But many monkeys rely on their

parents for several years, and ape kids take even longer to grow up. Chimps depend on their moms for five years, and gorillas hang around for even longer. In their long childhood, ape and monkey kids learn the skills they need to thrive as

adults. They don't sit reading "Learn arm swinging in a weekend" or "Amazon rain forest on $5 a day." Instead they learn as human babies do — by watching their parents and copying what they see.

No monkey business

They'd better pay close attention, because some of the social skills they learn could make the difference between survival and death. The main advantage of living in a group is safety. Monkeys are always in danger from other animals that would happily make a meal of them. Living in large groups is a form of self defense. With 50 pairs of eyes, a monkey group can be constantly on the lookout for predators (hunting animals) such as big cats, snakes, and large birds. When a loud screech warns of danger, the whole troop flees into the safety of the forest canopy.

Running away is the best defense for tree dwelling monkeys, but what do primates do if there's no forest? Monkeys that live in African grassland can't flee to a tree, nor can they call on a primate police posse, so they have to fend for themselves. When danger threatens baboons, they work together to ward off a predator. Their powerful teeth make handy weapons.

Sharing food and love

Living in a group isn't such a great idea when it comes to food. Much of the trouble and strife within a monkey group begins when food is hard to find. The strongest get first pick, but after that, monkeys don't always fight over who gets

the rest. Bonobos offer sex in exchange for food, but this is unusual. Other monkeys, such as vervets, share food with friends. By grooming each other, two females bond so that they can cooperate, rather than compete, for food. It's a little like saying "You cut my hair, and I'll do your homework."

Male primates also form alliances by grooming each

THE STRONG PROTECTIVE BOND BETWEEN A BABOON AND ITS MOTHER CONTINUES AFTER THE BABY BECOMES AN ADULT.

GROOMING DOES MORE THAN REMOVE DEAD SKIN AND ANNOYING INSECTS. IT KEEPS THE WHOLE APE FAMILY HAPPY.

other. A male monkey will groom a more powerful male in the hope that he will be given the chance to mate with a willing female. Male cooperation also extends to fighting – a weak male olive baboon strengthens a bond with a stronger male by helping him in a fight. The payoff comes when there are fertile females around – the stronger male will often let his fighting partner choose one of them as a mate.

Life is fun
Grooming primates concentrate so hard that they sometimes look as if they are working, but play is an important part of primate society, too. Chasing games are a favorite, whether on the ground or in trees, but great apes are more inventive. Chimps look for objects they can use as toys. The orange-sized fruit of the strychnos tree, for example, has a tough shell that makes it an ideal ball for throwing or rolling.

GROOMING IS COMMUNICATION THROUGH THE FINGERTIPS

59

Both adults and young primates play, but life is more carefree for the kids. They even play games with other species. A young chimp, for example, might pull the tail of a young baboon to start a rough-and-tumble game. Games end when the two are old enough to begin competing for food, and friends become rivals.

Y akety yak

Ape and monkey conversations are noisy, lively, multimedia affairs. To get a word in edgewise it's not enough to just chatter. You need to grimace, scowl, make faces, wave your arms and legs, and jump around as well. Sometimes there's no substitute for just shouting very loudly! The loudest of all primate calls are territorial. When howler or colobus monkeys, chimps, and gibbons yell out, they are telling everyone in hearing distance: "This is our piece of forest, find your own place." Alarm calls are noisy, too, because they have to reach friends and relatives who that are out of sight of danger.

Quieter calls keep monkeys and apes from getting separated. Female squirrel monkeys, for instance, make high-pitched calls when they stray from the gang. These "peeps" say "I'm here, so where are you?" Answering calls let them know they've not been forgotten.

P rimate talk

Communication really starts to get interesting, though, when it's up close and

IT'S HARD TO RESIST PLAYING WITH YOUR FOOD WHEN FRUIT MAKES A PERFECT BALL.

LOG ON...
www.indiana.
edu/~primate/primates.html

ORANGUTANS BUILD NESTS HIGH IN THE TREES FOR SLEEPING AT NIGHT, BUT MAY NAP ON THE GROUND DURING THE DAY.

personal. When primates can see each other, they use their faces to emphasize their words. Their faces are almost as flexible and muscular as our own, so they can move their eyes, ears, and mouths to add extra meaning to the noises they make. With sound and vision combined they express pleasure, fear, anger, excitement, and a whole range of other emotions.

Though these expressions can be similar to human ones, the meaning may be very different. Zoo monkeys, for example, seem to yawn a lot, but in "primatese" this wide-open-mouth expression is actually a warning, not a yawn.

Time for bed

As the sun sets, primates look for somewhere to sleep. They're experts at finding safe places, and as a result, they're the sleep champs of the animal world. They snooze almost as soundly as we do. Forest monkeys sleep in trees, while ground dwelling monkeys seek the protection of cliffs.

And where do baby apes sleep? Actually, both large and small apes build nests, a new one each day. Male gorillas nest on the ground. Because of their strength, they don't need the safety of trees, and because of their weight it's hard to find strong enough branches for a nest.

WEIRD WORLD
SCIENTISTS STUDY PRIMATE LANGUAGE TO GET CLOSE TO THEIR APE SUBJECTS. THEY HAVE FOUND THAT HOLDING OUT THE BACK OF THE HAND, FOR EXAMPLE, IS A FRIENDLY SIGN TO A CHIMP.

61

APES AND US

A group of chimps are watching a scientist who has followed them around all day. "If you half close your eyes, you would almost believe she was an ape" says one.

A GORILLA'S SKULL CAVITY SHOWS THE LARGE SIZE OF ITS BRAIN.

"Yes!" says another "... apparently you can teach them to swing from branches." "...and crack nuts in their teeth," adds a third. "Ah yes," says the wisest old chimp, "but you could never teach them how to find all the fruit trees and know when each one ripens."

Comparing us with them

If apes really did compare themselves to humans like this, all they'd care about would be our forest survival skills – and let's face it, we wouldn't get many checkmarks on their list. It's not really fair to compare – most people aren't built for jungle living – but we do just the same thing when we say "Apes aren't quite human."

Indeed, science books used to be packed full of reasons why humans are better than apes. Only humans smile and frown, laugh and cry, they said. Only humans walk upright, make tools, and have hands that can hold pens and swords, or thread needles. Only humans

WEIRD WORLD

JUST LIKE HUMANS, CHIMP GROUPS HAVE THEIR OWN CULTURES – LEARNED WAYS OF BEHAVING. CHIMPS IN ONE GROUP CAN HAMMER NUTS, FOR INSTANCE, WHILE A DIFFERENT GROUP HAVE NOT LEARNED THIS PARTICULAR TRICK.

can talk. As one 19th-century scientist put it "Between man and brutes there is an impassable barrier, over which man can never fall, or beasts hope to climb." If he was alive today, the barrier would not seem so high.

Chimpanzees

All apes make sounds of one kind or another, but until recently, scientists believed that humans were the only ape species that could actually speak. Now few deny that chimpanzees can learn to talk. Some even hold conversations with their keepers! The words they use don't come from their mouths, however. Chimps don't have the voicebox that's needed for human speech, so they have to communicate another way.

They do it with sign language. A female chimp called Washoe was the first to talk to her trainers by signing. In about 1966 American psychologists Beatrice and Allan Gardner taught Washoe to make some of the hand signs used by speech-and hearing-handicapped people.

CHIMPS USE TWIGS, LEAVES, AND STONES TO GET AND PREPARE FOOD, TO FAN AND SCRATCH THEMSELVES, AND IN MANY OTHER WAYS.

BONOBOS SUCH AS KANZI AND PANBANISHA (SHOWN HERE) LEARNED TO "TALK" BY POINTING AT SIGNS ON A BOARD.

Learning skills

In four years Washoe learned more than 150 words and combined them to form simple sentences. Most of them were demands for food – for example, "want berry."

Since then, other researchers have taught chimps to talk by pointing to signs on boards or by typing on special keyboards called lexigram keyboards. What did they say? You guessed it – they wanted food.

Ordering meals from a menu may not seem very impressive, but admit it – when you take a trip abroad, do you get any further than "what to eat" in the foreign language phrasebook?

Clever Kanzi

Kanzi, a bonobo taught by Sue

A FEW OF KANZI'S SIGNS, SUCH AS "YES" AND "QUESTION" MEAN SOMETHING TO US, BUT MOST ARE JUST BOLD SHAPES.

HELLO

YES

TICKLE

1 2 3 4 5

KANZI LEARNED TO PICK OUT SYMBOLS FROM A TOTAL OF 256. THIS CHART SHOWS HALF OF THE BRIGHTLY COLORED SIGNS.

Savage-Rumbaugh, was smarter at this game than a two-year-old child. Like Washoe, he made simple sentences such as "put the apple in the hat" by pointing at signs in the right order. He was also very smart about understanding spoken instructions. Most impressive of all, Kanzi learned his communication skills without constantly being "bribed" with food. Left to make up his own sentences, what did Kanzi ask for? Well, games such as "chase Kanzi" came near the top of the list. But the favorite – you guessed it – was more fruit.

Using tools

Chimps can learn to talk, but can they use tools? Until about 40 years ago people believed that making and using tools were unique human skills. What a shame they didn't ask the chimps for their opinion. Chimps make their lives easier with a variety of tools. They

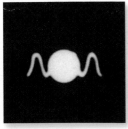

FOOD

QUESTION

LIGHT

A LEAF SPONGE SOAKED IN WATER QUENCHES A CHIMP'S THIRST QUICKER THAN WETTING AND LICKING IT.

their own tools. Here's how.

Chimps love termites, which are tricky to catch and eat. So, chimps do it by making a special fishing tool. They strip the leaves from a twig to make a short stick, which they poke into holes in a termite mound. Termites cling to it and – yum! – that's lunch.

Chimps rule, o.k? What about the other skills that are supposed to make humans superior? Well, apes may not cry, but they do have expressive faces, which show emotions in other

DNA "FINGERPRINTS" MEASURE JUST HOW ALIKE APES AND HUMANS AR

use leaves to wipe their hands (and butts). They crack nuts with carefully chosen hammer stones. By making "sponges" with chewed leaves they soak up water – then squeeze it into their mouths to drink.

Individually, none of these tricks are a big deal. Many animals use tools – vultures crack ostrich eggs with rocks, for example. But chimps make

ways. Humans walk upright, and our knuckles don't drag on the ground – but what's so special about that? In a human city an ape's four-legged trot would be out of place. But, in the forest, it's a different story. The agility of a chimp or gibbon puts the most athletic human to shame.

And the hand thing? Maybe apes can't hold a pen, but

secretarial skills are hardly in demand in the African rain forest. And it doesn't seem right to call an ape inferior because it can't thread a needle.

Measuring similarities

Apes are able to do all these humanlike things, but can we actually measure how human they are? Scientists think they can get some of the answers from DNA (deoxyribonucleic acid), a chemical found in all living things. DNA is a kind of code for life, describing plants and animals in every detail. The more similar an animal is to a human, the more of its DNA matches ours. So DNA is the closest thing we have to a "human meter."

Measured on this scale, the good news is that chimpanzees share 98 percent of our DNA. Does this mean they're 98 parts human and just two parts animal? Well, not exactly,

LOG ON...
http://chimp.st-ac.uk/cultures/links.htm

BY WATCHING THEIR ELDERS, YOUNG CHIMPS LEARN HOW TO LURE TASTY TERMITES WITH A PROBING STICK.

because here's the bad news. Even slugs and snails share half our DNA. So if chimps are 98 parts human, we're all half slug.

Man or monkey?

Apes are so similar to humans that some people believe we should treat them just the same as humans. Well, perhaps we already do. Street and circus performers found out long ago that they could make money from the similarity between primates and people. They dressed tame monkeys and apes in clothes and taught them tricks to please the crowds of people who came to see them. What could be more charming,

IN MALAYSIA MACAQUES ARE TRAINED TO CLIMB COCONUT PALMS AND THROW DOWN FRUIT TO THE FARMER BELOW.

DANCING TO MUSIC IS NOT NATURAL MONKEY BEHAVIOR

more human, than a chimp that eats with a knife and fork? Or a capuchin that collects money in a hat for the street musician?

These primates may be copying human behavior, but they are not being treated like humans. Teaching primates to do tricks usually involves punishment, and often mutilation of the animal. Circus trainers sometimes pull out their monkeys' teeth to stop them from biting.

The natural environment for primates is the forest, and forcing them to live and behave as humans do is unnatural, wrong, and unnecessary. And last but not least, taking primates from the wild for the purpose of entertainment endangers their survival.

Animal rights and wrongs

Really treating primates as

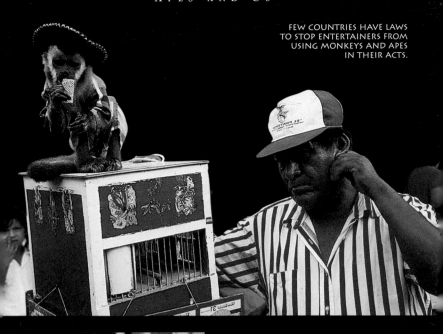

FEW COUNTRIES HAVE LAWS TO STOP ENTERTAINERS FROM USING MONKEYS AND APES IN THEIR ACTS.

humans would mean giving them the same rights as people, such as the right to life and liberty. This sounds like a great idea, but it's important to remember that as well as rights, humans have responsibilities – such as not harming others. Chimpanzees are strong enough to injure or even kill people. How would human laws deal with primate criminals who couldn't defend themselves or understand what they'd done? Nobody has yet found a good answer.

INTEREST GROUPS IN A VARIETY OF COUNTRIES ORGANIZE PROTESTS AGAINST THE USE OF ANIMALS IN RESEARCH.

PRIMATE RESEARCH

Tormented by insects and blood-sucking leeches, spattered with ape pee and stiff with muscle cramps, the life of a field primatologist isn't an easy ride. Don't let the name mislead you. The "field" part is a trick. These scientists don't spend lazy hours in fields of golden wheat or sweet-smelling hay studying monkeys and apes. "Field" really means "as far as you can get from the comforts of home and laboratory" — such as clean, dry clothes, hot showers, and flushing toilets.

What a life

Primatologists put up with these hardships for weeks, months, and years on end. Why do they do it? Ask 20 primatologists this question and you'll probably get a hundred different answers, but you'll also hear several reasons mentioned over and over again.

The spirit of inquiry

There's a lot we don't yet understand about monkeys and apes. We know most about species that live in grasslands, such as baboons, because they are easy to see and study. But forest-dwelling primates are hard to find and watch, and just

IN BRAZIL, IN 1987, DUTCH BIOLOGIST MARC
VAN ROOSEMALEN DISCOVERED THE TINY
BLACK-CROWNED DWARF MARMOSET.

IN BRAZIL, IN 1987, DUTCH BIOLOGIST MARC
VAN ROOSEMALEN DISCOVERED THE TINY
BLACK-CROWNED DWARF MARMOSET.

about impossible to follow
when they flee through the
forest canopy. Primatologists
have a mission to fill the
knowledge gap about these
rare, shy, and often hard-to-
spot animals.

D iscovering new apes

Stubborn scientists who stick it
out in the field are sometimes
richly rewarded. Not with
money, but with the buzz of
discovering a new species. In
just three years, for example,
scientists working in Brazil
found three new primate
species, including the Rio
Maués marmoset which
Marco Schwartz, a Swiss
primatologist, spotted in 1985.
A new monkey species is a big
deal and makes headlines in
scientific journals.

STUDYING ANIMAL BEHAVIOR IN THE
WILD INVOLVES HOURS OF PATIENT
OBSERVATION AND CAREFUL NOTE TAKING.

Vital research

Another reason for becoming a primatologist is that primates have problems. The bigger the primate, the bigger the problem. Some species are on the brink of extinction (dying out in the wild). Primate research is vital so that we know how many remain. It also helps us to work out ways to protect primates and increase their numbers. If we can't do this, our grandchildren may only see gorillas on TV.

You won't get rich

Primatologists – like many other scientists – certainly don't do the job for the money. Most research projects are supported by charities, universities, and government grants, and they don't have lots of cash to hand out.

It's the buzz

Perhaps the most important reason that people study primates in the forest – especially the great apes – is the thrill of working with these

RESEARCH IS VITAL TO SAVE APES FROM EXTINCTION

intelligent, social animals. Observing apes involves getting to know them. Every ape has a unique personality. Field workers know them and name them. They celebrate when their subjects give birth, and mourn when they die.

PLAY FIGHTING MAY BE FUN FOR A YOUNG CHIMP, BUT FOR A WATCHING PRIMATOLOGIST IT'S ALL PART OF A DAY'S WORK.

What do they do?

It sounds as if primatologists spend their time holding birthday parties. They certainly don't. Most of their time in the field they spend in observation. Very early each morning they set off into the forest, following muddy tracks worn by pigs or baboons. They take with them a watch,

SCIENTISTS STILL HAVE MUCH TO DISCOVER ABOUT THE ORANGUTAN, AND THEY HAVE LITTLE TIME LEFT: EXTINCTION MAY BE ONLY 10 YEARS AWAY.

notebook and pencil, binoculars, and a camera – and maybe a video camcorder. They watch, time, and record everything the animals do. To see anything at all, they may have to clamber up to the treetops. Primate species that spend their time high in the forest canopy are difficult to see from the ground.

Great ape researchers get close to their subjects and mingle. Chimps, bonobos, and gorillas are timid and stand-offish at first, but they gradually get used to the presence of human

Sifting through the evidence

When primatologists return to their laboratories and offices they analyze their findings and try to draw conclusions. From their records of what individual primates eat, they learn about the diet of the whole species. Counting the animals in a small area makes it possible to estimate the number remaining in a whole region. And from a study of a few pregnancies and births, primatologists calculate breeding rates – and predict likely future populations. Analysis of DNA in the laboratory enables them to

CAPTIVE AND WILD PRIMATES BEHAVE VERY DIFFERENTLY

CHIMPS HAVE PERSONALITIES SO LIKE OUR OWN THAT IT'S HARDLY SURPRISING SCIENTISTS GIVE THEM NAMES.

companions. Being accepted as "one of the troop" makes it easier for primatologists to get close to their subjects and observe. However, it has led to unexpected and even unwelcome discoveries. Anyone who imagines that all apes are cuddly is in for a surprise.

JANE GOODALL'S RESERVE BECAME HER
HOME AS WELL AS THAT OF HER CHIMPS.

trace how animals are related to
each other – and how far males
travel to find mates.

Some primatologists never
leave the laboratory. Many
who study primate
communication, for example,
can work only with captive
primates because they need
to have the animal's full
attention. In the wild,
chimps such as Washoe and
Kanzi would probably learn
to sign only "lesson boring,
I'm off" before heading out
of here into the trees.

75

Chimp champ

Primate research advances through the patient efforts of thousands of scientists, but two primate researchers have attracted particular attention. They are famous for their discoveries about chimps and gorillas, and for their dedication to their research over many years.

From childhood, British researcher Jane Goodall (born 1934) was fascinated by animals. At the age of four she hid in a chicken house to see where eggs came from. She sat still and silent for hours. Eventually Jane saw a hen lay an egg, and she learned an important lesson – patience is essential in any research.

In 1960, Jane began studying chimpanzees at Gombe Stream Game Reserve (now a national park) in Tanzania. She thought her work would take three years, but it's still going on. It has become the world's longest study of animals in the wild.

Jane's first important discovery was that chimps eat meat – until then, everyone thought they were vegetarian. She made the first records of chimp warfare, tool making, cannibalism, partnerships, and the use of healing plants.

Jane no longer works at Gombe. She campaigns for better conditions for laboratory primates, for the establishment of chimp sanctuaries, and for forest conservation.

Primatologist in the mist

Like Jane Goodall, Dian Fossey (1932-85) studied African apes. In the Virunga Mountains of

JANE GOODALL'S DISCOVERY THAT CHIMPS MAKE TOOLS HELPED ESTABLISH HER AS A LEADING CHIMP RESEARCHER.

LOG ON...
www.gre...
org/gap...me.html
...eproject.

SIGOURNEY WEAVER PLAYED DIAN FOSSEY IN THE FILM VERSION OF HER BOOK.

Rwanda she spent nearly 20 years watching rare mountain gorillas. As a result of her studies she became the world's greatest expert on these shy animals. Her best-selling book, *Gorillas in the Mist*, made her a hero among conservationists. Dian Fossey was impatient with those who disagreed with her, and her personality and methods earned her many enemies. When farming and hunting threatened the gorillas she thought of as her family, she fought back – and paid with her life. She was murdered in 1985.

In the lab

Not all primate research benefits the animals. Because their bodies are so like our own, captive primates can take the place of humans in experiments. For example, before the National Aeronautics and Space Administration (NASA) risked launching a human astronaut in 1961, it sent into space a rocket carrying a chimp called Ham.

Today, most laboratory primates are used to study human disease. Some research projects have worthwhile goals, such as finding cures for deadly diseases. Medical research would be more difficult without the use of primates. Chimps were thought to be ideal for this research, because they can catch these diseases without becoming ill.

In well-run research facilities, apes and monkeys are well-treated. Nevertheless, primates used for medical research don't always live a natural existence. Often they are isolated to prevent infection. Because of this, and because some labs don't look after primates as well as they should, there is a certain amount of opposition to laboratory tests involving monkeys and apes.

FAREWELL TO APES

How many jumbo jets would it take to carry all the mountain gorillas in the world? A thousand? A hundred maybe? Try again. As long as they took up only one seat each (and didn't fight over who sat by the windows), you could load them all onto two aircraft.

Disappearing gorillas

There are probably only 600 mountain gorillas left – just two-thirds of the number that were alive 40 years ago. Although conservation efforts have now stopped numbers from falling, these magnificent apes are dangerously close to being wiped out.

No other primate is in such peril, but other species are also threatened. Unless primates have more protection, many will become extinct (die out) by the end of the century. Why? It's a long, sad story of greed, hunger, and despair.

Felling the forests

Most monkeys and apes live in the tropical rain forests of South and Central America,

CIVIL WAR IN THE DEMOCRATIC REPUBLIC OF CONGO KILLED AS MANY AS HALF OF ALL GORILLAS THAT ONCE LIVED THERE.

Africa, and Southeast Asia. These lush, wet, green woodlands once covered a fifth of the Earth's surface, but they are shrinking rapidly. Less than half of all natural rain forest remains standing, and an area the size of Greece or North Carolina is cleared each year. Very poor people are responsible for some of the rain forest destruction. To hungry humans, forests seem like wastelands (the word "jungle" means desert in one

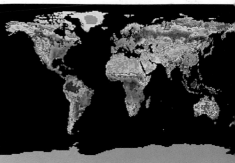

RAIN FOREST AREAS WHERE PRIMATES LIVE (DARK GREEN ON THIS MAP) ARE BEING DESTROYED VERY RAPIDLY.

Indian language). So they cut down the trees for firewood or to farm the land.

Unfortunately, rain forest soils are poor, and crops grow on them for only a few years. When the soil is exhausted, farmers move on and cut down more forest – making more primates homeless.

Monkey meat
People living in and around the rain forests harm monkeys and apes more directly – by hunting them. They either eat

WEIRD WORLD
NOBODY KNOWS FOR SURE HOW MANY PRIMATES HUNTERS KILL, BUT IN WEST AND CENTRAL AFRICA, 3,000 GORILLAS AND 4,000 CHIMPS MAY DIE EACH YEAR. THAT'S MORE THAN ALL THE CAPTIVE ANIMALS IN THE WORLD.

the animals or sell them as "bushmeat" in towns, which goes for as much as best steak. As long as there were many monkeys and apes and a few humans, hunting didn't matter. But now that there are more humans and fewer primates, the bushmeat business threatens the survival of some primates.

There's a trade in live monkeys and apes, too. Scientists buy primates to use in experiments, and the smaller monkeys make appealing pets. Young animals are most in demand, and hunters who spot a monkey family will kill the protective mother in order to capture her children.

War makes primate hunters even more desperate. Some African rain forests are in war zones where fighting has driven people from their homes in the forest. Conservation is a luxury these hungry and poor refugees can't afford. For them, the alternative to a monkey hunt may be an empty belly or death.

HUNTERS TRAP AND SPEAR PRIMATES, BUT MORE USE GUNS. HUNTING IS COMMON IN WAR ZONES WHERE PEOPLE CARRY ARMS.

Getting rich in the forest

As the world's poor nibble away at primates and their homes, greedy businessmen take great bites out of the rain forest. Trees such as mahogany are very valuable. Lumber companies fell the precious trees to make furniture and building materials. Oil and mining companies destroy the rain forest, too, as they hunt and extract underground minerals.

All these activities cut down primate habitat (in other words, suitable living space).

LOG ON...
http://bushmeat./net
www.peta-online.org

THOUGH TRADE IN LIVE CHIMPS IS NOW ILLEGAL, A HUNTER WILL STILL KILL A MOTHER TO CAPTURE AND SELL HER YOUNG AS PETS.

Save a monkey, save a tree

Saving primate species from extinction is not easy. The only sure way to do it is protecting their forest habitat. Not everyone agrees how – or even whether – we should save the rain forests. The noisiest opponents are the loggers, farmers, miners, and oil drillers who make huge profits by exploiting them. They have proposed many alternative ways to save primates. Here are a couple of the silliest.

Keep them in zoos

Opponents of forest conservation suggest that we keep all the world's primates alive in zoos and wildlife parks. This just isn't practical. Primates are wild animals, and while some thrive and breed in captivity, others sicken and die. Even if we found ways of keeping all primates healthy and happy in cages and compounds, there simply wouldn't be enough zoos to hold them all. You can't breed a troop of healthy animals from just one or two pairs, because the weaknesses of adult animals are concentrated in their young. Captive breeding programs work best when many animals breed, so that defects are diluted (made less strong) with each generation.

Let's just clone them!

In the movie *Jurassic Park*, scientists bring back to life a long-extinct dinosaur by cloning (copying over and over) the DNA in a drop of its preserved blood. Real life cloning has produced identical "photocopy" sheep. So why don't we just store the DNA of the remaining endangered

81

mountain gorillas, then clone them when they are all extinct? This seems like an attractive idea, and cloning may help captive breeding programs in the future. But as an alternative to conservation, it simply doesn't work. Cloning is very slow and would be pointless if there were no forests into which the cloned animals could be released.

The world's last wilderness Preserving what remains of the world's rain forest is without a doubt the key to the long-term survival of primates – and of countless other species of animals and plants, too.

To be really effective, rain forest conservation must preserve large, continuous areas of forest, and include all the trees within it. Small pockets of rain forest are of little value. There is not enough food and space in each one to support a troop of monkeys big enough to breed. Escaping to areas of nearby forest is often impossible because the cleared land all around is too wide for primates to cross safely.

RANGERS NOW GUARD GORILLAS OF THE VIRUNGA MOUNTAINS, BUT THEY ARE TOO FEW AND POACHERS STILL KILL ANIMALS.

LOGGING DESTROYS RAIN FOREST FOREVER, BECAUSE IT DRIVES OUT THE ANIMALS THAT SPREAD THE SEEDS OF GIANT TREES.

Even selective logging – where only a few trees are felled – causes changes to rain forests that cannot be reversed. The tallest trees make the most valuable timber, but these very trees provide homes and food for a unique community of forest creatures. For example, red colobus, black and white colobus, and diana monkeys live in the tops of Africa's highest trees. Felling just these trees for timber endangers the monkeys that rely on them.

COUNTRIES WHERE APES LIVE PRINT THEM ON MONEY, BUT WON'T SPEND IT ON PROTECTING THEM.

83

What can I do?

Perhaps it's hard to see how you can protect primates or their rain forest homes, but there are ways in which you can help. Here are a few.

• Don't go to events that use primates. Though a few trainers treat their animals humanely, many do not. Your ticket money helps encourage the capture and trade in young apes and monkeys that are believed suitable for showbiz, fairground, and circus stunts.

• Find out about joining an organization that campaigns for the protection of primates or for the fair treatment of animals

People for the Ethical Treatment of Animals (PETA)

This group campaigns against animal cruelty and abuse.
www.peta-online.org
501 Front Street
Norfolk, VA 23510

Worldwide Fund for Nature (WWF)

World's largest conservation organization. Visit the website to check out the Living Planet Report.
www.panda.org
1250 24th Street NW
Washington, DC 20037-1175

• Ask your parents not to buy furniture made of mahogany. Lumber trade organizations such as the Rainforest Alliance Smart Wood Program can guarantee that furniture is not made from wood plundered from the rain forest.

At least if you do just one of the above, you will know you are helping to preserve the world's primates.

WITHOUT YOUR HELP, SOME OF THE WORLD'S MOST FANTASTIC ANIMALS MAY DIE IN THE WILD.

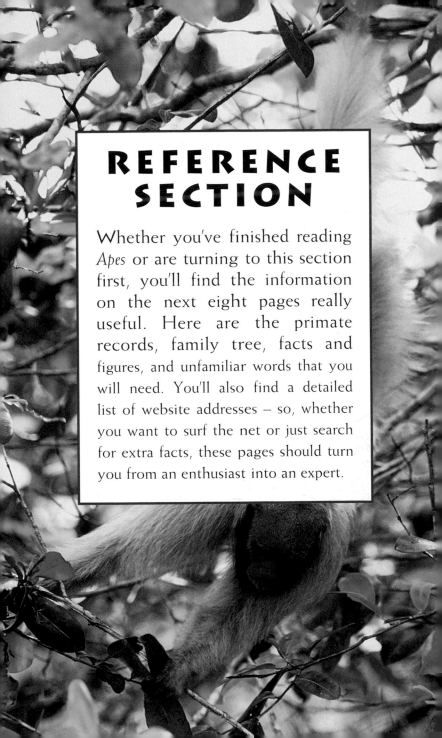

REFERENCE SECTION

Whether you've finished reading *Apes* or are turning to this section first, you'll find the information on the next eight pages really useful. Here are the primate records, family tree, facts and figures, and unfamiliar words that you will need. You'll also find a detailed list of website addresses – so, whether you want to surf the net or just search for extra facts, these pages should turn you from an enthusiast into an expert.

PRIMATE CLASSIFICATION

In order to discuss all the different species of plant and animal, scientists classify them into a series of categories according to the features that they share. The largest category is the kingdom. Primates are part of the animal kingdom, which also includes every other animal species. The kingdom is divided into smaller categories, which are further divided until individual species are reached. The smaller the category, the more features the animals have in common. This chart shows the classification of the chimpanzee.

Kingdom: animal
Unlike living things in other kingdoms, animals can move freely. The animal kingdom includes more than 30 phyla.

Phylum: chordata
Most members of the chordata phylum are vertebrates – beasts with backbones. The phylum includes nine classes of animal.

Class: mammalia
Like all other mammals, chimps produce milk to feed their young. The mammalia class includes about 20 different orders.

Order: primates
Most primates have large brains, short noses, and versatile, gripping hands and feet. There are 12 families of primates.

Family: pongidae
Usually called the great apes, the pongidae family includes not only the chimpanze, but also the orangutan and gorilla.

Genus: pan
This genus includes two primate species: the chimpanzee and bonobo.

Species: troglodytes
The chimp's scientific name means "cave dweller". Within this one species there are three "races": common, masked, and eastern chimps.

What is a species?
A species is the basic unit of classification. A species is a group of similar animals that are capable of breeding together in the wild to produce fertile offspring.

PROSIMIAN FAMILIES

This chart gives details of the six prosimian families. Prosimians have a special importance – the distant ancestor of humans and all other primates was a prosimian like a lemur. Today, lemurs and many other prosimians are found only on the African island of Madagascar, so they are specially at risk of extinction. Five of the ten most endangered primates are prosimians from the island.

NAME	MEANING	EXAMPLES	SPECIES	FEATURES
Tupaiidae	Squirrel-like	Tree shrews	15	Live in Southeast Asian forests, on ground and in trees. Family includes smallest primate.
Lemuridae	Ghost/spirit of the dead	Lemurs	14	Group-living, slender primates, cat-size or smaller. Active at night; found only on East African islands.
Indriidae	"There it is"	Indri, avahi, sifakas	4	Long-legged Madagascan tree-dwellers. Cling and leap expertly.
Daubentoniidae	Named for naturalist Louis Daubenton (1716–1800)	Aye-aye	1	Rare, solitary, squirrel-like tree-dweller from Madagascar. Hunts insects at night.
Lorisidae	Clown	Lorises potto galagos	12	Tree-dwellers of India, Southeast Asia and mainland Africa.
Tarsiidae	Long foot	Tarsiers	3	Goggle-eyed insect eater of Southeast Asia.

PRIMATE RECORDS

Biggest and smallest
•The eastern lowland gorilla is the tallest and heaviest primate. In the wild, males grow to 5 ft 10 in (1.8m) or so and typically weigh 375 lb (170 kg). Animals in zoos get even heavier (through lack of exercise) and some weigh up to 660 lb (300 kg).
•The largest monkey is the mandrill – males weigh about 71 lb (32 kg).
•The smallest monkey is the pygmy marmoset. Adults weigh about 2 oz (60 g) – roughly the same as 20 sugar lumps.
•The smallest primate is a prosimiam, the pen-tailed tree shrew, which is about half the weight of a pygmy marmoset.

Long life
•The longest-lived of all primates is the chimpanzee. In captivity, some survive into their 50s, and one lived to be 59.

Distribution
•Macaques are the most adaptable of all primates. They have spread throughout southern Asia, and as far west as Gibraltar, at the southwestern corner of Europe. Of the macaques, Rhesus macaques are the most widespread, living from Afghanistan to Vietnam.

Most intelligent
Intelligence in primates is difficult to measure, but chimpanzees are probably the most intelligent of all, except for humans.
•Among the monkeys, baboons take the record for brains.

Fastest and slowest
•On the ground, the fastest moving primate is probably the patas monkey, which can race at speeds of 35 mph (55 kmh).
•The slowest is a prosimian, the slow loris. Special muscles enable it to keep perfectly still, but prevent it from running, even when frightened.

Noisiest
•Howler monkeys are the noisiest primate. They are the loudest land animal, too. Their calls can be heard up to 10 miles (16 km) away.

Breeding rates
•The orangutan is the slowest breeder of all primates. Females give birth about every eight years, and may have only three or four young in their lives.
•Generally, smaller primates breed faster, so it's no surprise that the mouse lemur is one of the fastest. Pregnancy lasts just two months.

THREATS TO PRIMATES

Threat	Region of danger	Threatened animals
Forest clearance for farming	Madagascar → Central and South America →	Lemurs, sifakas; Many New World monkeys
Industrial logging	Southeast Asia → Central and South America →	Orangutans; Many New World monkeys
Fuel wood collection	West and Central Africa, Madagascar →	Chimpanzees and gorillas, sifakas and lemurs
Hunting for food and traditional medicine	West and Central Africa, Vietnam →	Larger primates that can provide a lot of meat – chimpanzees and gorillas, drills, langurs
Live trapping for medical research, pets, and entertainment	Hunters in Southeast Asian and African countries supply animals mainly to the USA and UK →	Chimpanzees and gorillas, orangutans, and gibbons
Mining – disturbance drives monkeys out; workers hunt primates	Central Africa → Madagascar → Amazonia →	Gorillas; Sifakas, lemurs; Many New World monkeys
Oil exploration and drilling	Amazonia →	Many New World monkeys
Warfare – refugees hunt primates for food	Central Africa →	Gorillas

MOST ENDANGERED

Roughly half of all primate species are endangered. So perhaps it is unfair to single out one species of ape or monkey for special attention. However, measured by primate numbers in the wild, the Tonkin snub-nose langur of Vietnam is closest to extinction – there may be only 200 of them left.

APES GLOSSARY

Agile
Able to move quickly and easily with little effort.

Aggression
Threatening or destructive behavior.

Alpha male
The most powerful male that controls an animal group.

Bacteria
Tiny creatures that cause decay or disease in plants and animals.

Brachiation
Swinging by the arms from branch to branch.

Cannibal
An animal that lives by feeding on animals of the same kind.

Carnivore
An animal that eats meat. May also eat plants.

Cellulose
A tough material from which plant cell walls are built.

Colony
A group of animals living together, protecting and supporting each other.

Cooperative
A mutual willingness to help.

Culture
Patterns of behavior that members of a group share.

Diet
The variety of food that an animal eats.

DNA
Short for deoxyribonucleic acid, a long, spiral-shape chemical found in all living things. Plants and animals pass on their characteristics to their offspring by transferring DNA during reproduction.

Double-jointed
Having very flexible joints between bones.

Environment
The natural world in which all life on Earth exists, or the particular conditions of plant and animal life at one place.

Evolution
The gradual process by which living things change or improve. Animals that are better in some way than their siblings are more likely to survive and pass this ability on to their offspring.

Extinction
The end of a particular kind of living thing, when the last example of it on Earth dies.

Field research
Study that takes a scientist out of the laboratory or office.

Forage
To search for food.

Forest canopy
The dense layer of leaves at the top of the tallest forest trees.

Gland
Part of an animal's body that makes natural chemicals to control bodily functions.

Grooming
Cleaning of the body to remove dirt or harmful creatures.

Habitat
The surroundings and natural resources that a plant or animal needs for living.

Herbivore
An animal that feeds on plants and does not eat meat.

Hierarchy
A setup in which a few powerful individuals control a larger number of weaker ones – who in turn control those weaker still.

Hominid
A human being or one of our apelike ancestors.

Interest group
A group of people who join together to put pressure on politicians to make changes.

Intestines
The lower part of the gut.

Mammal
Any member of a group of warm-blooded, mainly furry animals with backbones, which give birth to live young and feed them with their milk.

Monogamous
Living and breeding with just one partner.

New World monkeys
Monkeys from North, Central, and South America.

Nocturnal
Active at night.

Old World monkeys
Monkeys from Africa and Asia.

Opposable thumb
A thumb that can be moved across the fingers, to grip tightly.

Pair bond
An exclusive relationship, between two breeding animals.

Pellet
A small rounded object that is excreted by an animal.

Pot-bellied
Having an enlarged, rounded stomach.

Predator
An animal that hunts other animals for food.

Prehensile
Capable of gripping. From Latin *bendere*, meaning "to grasp."

Primate
A monkey or ape.

Primatologist
A scientist who studies primates.

Prosimian
A group of primates that are like monkeys, but less developed.

Protein
A kind of food that animals need for growth and healing of muscles and other body tissue.

Range
To move within a restricted area, often in search of food.

Rivals
Individuals that compete for scarce resources, such as food, water, or mates.

Signing
Communicating silently using signals made with the hands.

Silverback
Mature male gorilla.

Species
A group of animals or plants that share many features that together make them different from other plants or animals.

Stalk
To follow carefully and secretly when hunting.

Tannins
Bitter chemicals that are present in unripe fruit.

Territory
An area controlled by an animal or by a group of them.

PRIMATE ORGANIZATIONS

The Leakey Foundation
Named after the famous anthropologist Louis Leakey, the foundation
sponsors and organizes research related to behavior and survival.
www.leakeyfoundation.org/
PO Box 29346, 1002A O'Reilly Avenue
San Francisco, CA 94129-0346
Email: info@leakeyfoundation.org

Conservation International
The objectives of Conservation International are to conserve the
Earth's living natural heritage and global biodiversity, and to
demonstrate that human societies can live in harmony with nature.
www.conservation.org/

Gorilla Foundation
The main aim of the Gorilla Foundation is to promote the protection,
preservation, and breeding of gorillas. The foundation also has a
program for teaching sign language to gorillas.
www.gorilla.org/

Dian Fossey Gorilla Fund
Founded by the famous researcher Dian Fossey, DFGF is
dedicated to the conservation and protection of gorillas and their
habitat in Africa. The fund helps local communities in the region
through education and training, and promotes research and education
about gorillas.
www.gorillafund.org/

Orangutan Foundation United States
Branch of the Orangutan Foundation International (OFI). The
foundation's aim is to support the conservation and understanding of
the orangutan and its rain forest habitat while caring for ex-captive
individuals as they make their way back to the forest.
www.orangutan.org

822 S. Wellesley Ave.,
Los Angeles, CA 90049
Email: info@orangutan.org

Jane Goodall Institute (JGI)

Founded by the well-known chimp researcher, the institute aims to increase our knowledge and understanding of chimpanzees and other primates. It promotes the protection of chimps and the conservation of their habitat, and encourages research that will help them.

www.janegoodall.org/
P.O.Box 14890
Silver Spring,
MD 20911-4890

Primate Society of Great Britain

A scientific society that promotes research into all aspects of primate biology, conservation, and management.

www.psgb.org/

Forest Stewardship Council

This international organization based in Mexico supports the conservation of the world's forests through responsible management. It coordinates labeling programs for forest products throughout the world. The council's name and symbol on a wooden item guarantees that the product comes from a well-managed forest.

www.fscoax.org/

ADDITIONAL PRIMATE LINKS

Great Ape Project

Legal rights and protection for the great apes.

www.greatapeproject.org/

Primate Info Net

A comprehensive website for anyone with an interest in the primates.

www.primate.wisc.edu/pin/

Electronic Zoo

A site that also features other animal and veterinary information.

netvet.wustl.edu/primates.htm

Fieldwork

A personal page by a scientist who studies chimpanzees.

http://php.indiana.edu/~kdhunt/fieldwork.html

INDEX

CREDITS

Dorling Kindersley would like to thank: Almudena Diaz and Nomazwe Madonko for their DTP assistance, and Chris Bernstein for compiling the index.

Additional photography:
Peter Anderson, Geoff Brightling, Peter Chadwick, Geoff Dann, Dave King, Alan Watson, and Jerry Young.

Picture Credits

The publishers would like to thank the following for their kind permission to reproduce their photographs:
c = center; b = bottom;
l = left; r = right; t = top.

Ancient Art & Architecture Collection: 10-11, 11cl.
Bruce Coleman Ltd: A Compost 61tl;
Bruce Coleman Inc. 1, 41tc, 43tl;
C Zuber 8tr; Christen Fredriksson 38tr; Jorg and Petra Wegner 14, 51bc; Luiz Claudio Marigo 85; Paul Van Gaalen 57tc; Rod Williams 13br; Uwe Walz 54.
Environmental Images: Pete Addis 69bl.
Mary Evans Picture Library: 15bc.
Language Centre, Georgia State University, Atlanta: 64bc; 64tc; 65.
The Jane Goodall Institute - UK: Baron Hugo van Lawick 75tc; 75tr.
Ronald Grant Archive: 15tc; Warner Bros 77tl.
Robert Harding Picture Library: Frans Lanting 33tl.
FLPA - Images of Nature: Frank W Lane 21tc, 88-89; Gerard Laci 84bl; Gerard Lucz 55tr; Mark Newman 19br; Silvestric Fotoservice 48; T Whittaker 6 bc,89;
N:H.P.A. : Ann & Steve Toon 58br, 81tl; Douglas Dickins 68tr; Gerard Lacz 30bc, 46tr, 50tc; Jany Sauvanet 69tc, 83tc; Nigel J Dennis 34tc; Steve Robinson 60bl.

Oxford Scientific Films: A & M Shah 37tc; A Plumptre 35, 59tc; Alan Root 47tl; Bob Bennett 52bc; C Bromhall 49tr; Daniel J Cox 24bc; Konrad Wothe 44; Michael Sewell 26tl; Mike Birkhead 18bc, 76-77; N Rosing 80-81; N Bromhall 39bc; Nick Gordon 7tr; Phil Devries 23br; Stan Osolinski 31tr, 32, 72bl.
Powerstock Photolibrary / Zefa: Crejun 74-75.
Dr Ian Redmond: Dian Fossey 70-71; Ian Redmond 16-17, 82bc.
Dr Marc G M van Roosmalen: 71tr.
Science Photo Library: George Holton 63; NASA/Goddard Institute for Space Studies 79tr; Tim Davis 67bc; Tom McHugh 66cla.
The Wildlife Collection: J Giustina 56bl, 76bc; 53tr.
University College: 62tl.
Woodfall Wild Images: Tom Murphy 36cr, 44-45.
Gunter Ziesler: 40br.

Book Jacket Credits
Front cover:
Gorilla by gettyimages stone
Back cover: tr
Young orangutan by Christer Fredriksson/Bruce Coleman
Back cover: bl
Silverback gorilla © Dorling Kindersley

All other images © Dorling Kindersley. For further information see:
www.dkimages.com